My First Riddle

Bristol & Somerset

Edited By Jess Giaffreda

First published in Great Britain in 2019 by:

Young Writers Est. 1991

Young Writers
Remus House
Coltsfoot Drive
Peterborough
PE2 9BF
Telephone: 01733 890066
Website: www.youngwriters.co.uk

FOREWORD

Dear Reader,

Are you ready to get your thinking caps on to puzzle your way through this wonderful collection?

Young Writers are proud to introduce our new poetry competition, *My First Riddle*, designed to introduce Reception pupils to the delights of poetry. Riddles are a great way to introduce children to the use of poetic expression, including description, similes and expanded noun phrases, as well as encouraging them to 'think outside the box' by providing clues without giving the answer away immediately. Some pupils were given a series of riddle templates to choose from, giving them a framework within which to shape their ideas.

Their answers could be whatever or whoever their imaginations desired; from people to places, animals to objects, food to seasons. All of us here at Young Writers believe in the importance of inspiring young children to produce creative writing, including poetry, and we feel that seeing their own riddles in print will ignite that spark of creativity.

We hope you enjoy riddling your way through this book as much as we enjoyed reading all the entries.

CONTENTS

Lottie Carpenter (4)	62
Esmae Williams-Dracup (4)	63

St Mary's CE Primary School, Timsbury

Imogen Sophie Holland (4)	64
Joshua Wills (4)	65
Daisy Miell (4)	66
Jenson Squire (5)	67
Finley Josh Humphries (5)	68

St Mary's CE Primary School, Yate

Toby Blake (5)	69
Cassie Grier (5)	70
Emelia Welsford (5)	71
Jonah Harris (4)	72
Eddie Fitton (4)	73
Alfie Pearce (5)	74
Robyn Ellen Gapper (5)	75
Archie Jones (4)	76
Zac De Nobriga (4)	77
Adalae Smith (5)	78
Mia Jane Wiltshire (5)	79
Samuel Shipp (5)	80
Sienna Hollister-Rushent (5)	81
Cali Jefferies (4)	82
Maisie Leach (4)	83
Mollie Matten (5)	84
Charlie Sivell (4)	85
Tayton Andrews (4)	86
Elizabeth Bird (4)	87
Mason-Lee Cahill (4)	88
Jack Sady (5)	89
Finley Thomas (5)	90
Ella Grace Stone (4)	91
Erin Bartlett (4)	92
Max Rivett (5)	93
Rosa Ellen Base (4)	94
Phoebe Miles (4)	95
Olivia Everson (5)	96
Elizabeth Gay (4)	97

Hattie Wilburn (4)	98
Isaac Blacket (5)	99
George Jago (5)	100

St Nicholas CE Primary School, Henstridge

Isabel Basson (4)	101
Isaac George New (4)	102
E Hancock (4)	103
Maddison Elliott (4)	104
Logan Sunley (5)	105
McKenzie Murphy (4)	106
Jake Stanley (5)	107
Kaydee-Leigh Amelie Downton (5)	108
Grace Windsor (5)	109
Archie Parsons (4)	110
Alfie McKenna (4)	111

Trinity Church Primary School, Radstock

Freddie Brown (5), Ada, Violet, Fynn & Henry	112
Jacob Shearn (4), Leo, Tobious Mark Edward Wightman (4) & Aron	113
Savannah Evans-Isaac (5), Amber, Alfred R (5), Riley & Orrv	114

Wansdyke Primary School, Whitchurch

Victor Posea (5)	115
Joey Chillcott (4)	116
Carter Tulloch (4)	117
Kaiyrian-Jay McKenzie West (4)	118
Albie White (4)	119
Renae Coulton (4)	120
Sienna Carnevale (5)	121
Kai Saunders (4)	122

Westover Green Community School, Westover Green

Lily Collins (5)	123
Lillie Pocock (5)	124
Rebecca Hook (5)	125
Azala Ashley Baker (4)	126
Jack Stark (4)	127
Lucy Lilyrose Newland (5)	128
Lilly-Rose German (4)	129
Jordan Davis (5)	130
Alisha-Marie Warren (5)	131
Jasper Brown (4)	132
Tobie-Jai Hammett (4)	133
Violet Brooks (4)	134
Jaylen Fursland (4)	135
Skajus Rapsevicius (4)	136
Kiowa Erkhagen (4)	137
Archie Locke (4)	138
Ella Skidmore (5)	139
Georgia Gibbs (4)	140
Carolina Nascimento-Carvalho (5)	141
Tayleanna Imogene Mattock-Westlake (4)	142
Ryvver Bastin (4)	143
Bella Marie Gardner (4)	144
Riley Saunders (4)	145
Ivy Rose Lewis (4)	146
Lyle Keats (5)	147
Destiny Demain (5)	148
Kian Edward James Langdon (4)	149
Isabela Lipinska (4)	150
Ana Menyhart (5)	151

THE
RIDDLES

Freya's First Riddle

Who could it be?
Follow the clues and see.

It looks **black and white**.
It sounds like **woof, woof**!
It smells **clean after a wash**.
It feels **soft and furry**.
It tastes like **chews and treats**.

Have you guessed who it could be?
Look below and you will see,
It is...

Answer: *Oscar the dog.*

Freya Williams (4)
Meadowbrook Primary School, Bradley Stoke

Adrianna's First Riddle

What could it be?
Follow the clues and see.

It looks like **a person**.
It sounds like *crunch, crunch*!
It smells like **ginger**.
It feels **hard**.
It tastes like **Christmas**.

Have you guessed what it could be?
Look below and you will see,
It is...

Answer: A gingerbread man.

Adrianna Green (4)
Meadowbrook Primary School, Bradley Stoke

Mira's First Riddle

What could it be?
Follow the clues and see.

It looks like **a stick**.
It sounds like **the wind**.
It smells like **mud and grass**.
It feels like **wood and paper**.
It tastes like **sand and dirt**.

Have you guessed what it could be?
Look below and you will see,
It is...

Answer: A tree.

Mira Samhan (4)
Meadowbrook Primary School, Bradley Stoke

Iola's First Riddle

What could it be?
Follow the clues and see.

It looks **round and green**.
It sounds like **crunch, crunch**!
It smells **sweet**.
It feels **soft and smooth**.
It tastes like **juice**.

Have you guessed what it could be?
Look below and you will see,
It is...

Answer: A grape.

Iola Dorrington-Webb (4)
Meadowbrook Primary School, Bradley Stoke

Chase's First Riddle

What could it be?
Follow the clues and see.

It looks like **black and orange stripes**.
It sounds like **a big roar**!
It smells like **green grass**.
It feels like **a furry rug**.
It tastes like **Frosties**.

Have you guessed what it could be?
Look below and you will see,
It is...

Answer: A tiger.

Chase Malpas (4)
Meadowbrook Primary School, Bradley Stoke

Yashwin's First Riddle

What could it be?
Follow the clues and see.

It looks like **a waterfall**.
It sounds like *pitter-patter*!
It smells like **soil**.
It feels like **water**.
It tastes like **drinking water**.

Have you guessed what it could be?
Look below and you will see,
It is...

Answer: *Rain.*

Yashwin Inampudi (4)
Meadowbrook Primary School, Bradley Stoke

Jack's First Riddle

What could it be?
Follow the clues and see.

It looks like **a square**.
It sounds like **ding-dong**!
It smells like **dinner**.
It feels like **stone**.
It tastes like **bricks**.

Have you guessed what it could be?
Look below and you will see,
It is...

Answer: A house.

Jack Battye (5)
Meadowbrook Primary School, Bradley Stoke

Isla-Rose's First Riddle

What could it be?
Follow the clues and see.

It looks like **a kitty.**
It sounds like **meow, meow!**
It smells like **dog treats.**
It feels **furry and soft.**
It tastes like **cat food.**

Have you guessed what it could be?
Look below and you will see,
It is...

Answer: A cat.

Isla-Rose Atwill (5)
Meadowbrook Primary School, Bradley Stoke

Pippa's First Riddle

What could it be?
Follow the clues and see.

It looks like **a bucket**.
It sounds like **crashing waves**.
It smells like **seaweed**.
It feels **soft**.
It tastes like **gritty ice cream**.

Have you guessed what it could be?
Look below and you will see,
It is...

Answer: A sandcastle.

Pippa Carr (4)
Meadowbrook Primary School, Bradley Stoke

Sophie's First Riddle

What could it be?
Follow the clues and see.

It looks like **a bald egg.**
It sounds like **a siren.**
It smells like **talcum powder.**
It feels like **a squishy.**
It tastes like **a cupcake.**

Have you guessed what it could be?
Look below and you will see,
It is...

Answer: A baby.

Sophie Mae Williams (4)
Meadowbrook Primary School, Bradley Stoke

Jeevan's First Riddle

What could it be?
Follow the clues and see.

It looks like **a light**.
It sounds like **shhh**!
It smells like **fresh flowers**.
It feels like **glass**.
It tastes like **flowers**.

Have you guessed what it could be?
Look below and you will see,
It is...

Answer: A candle.

Jeevan Dev Singh (4)
Meadowbrook Primary School, Bradley Stoke

Sienna's First Riddle

What could it be?
Follow the clues and see.

It looks like **melted snow**.
It sounds like **pouring**.
It smells like **cows**.
It feels **yummy and cold**.
It tastes like **cows and creamy**.

Have you guessed what it could be?
Look below and you will see,
It is...

Answer: Milk.

Sienna Swanston (4)
Meadowbrook Primary School, Bradley Stoke

Rig's First Riddle

What could they be?
Follow the clues and see.

They look like **a circle**.
They sound **crunchy**.
They smell **cheesy**.
They feel like **feathers**.
They taste **sweet and salty**.

Have you guessed what they could be?
Look below and you will see,
They are...

Answer: Crisps.

Rig Gupta (5)
Meadowbrook Primary School, Bradley Stoke

Amelia's First Riddle

What could it be?
Follow the clues and see.

It looks like **two pointy ears**.
It sounds like *meow*!
It smells like **fish**.
It feels like **soft fur**.
It tastes **yucky**.

Have you guessed what it could be?
Look below and you will see,
It is...

Answer: A cat.

Amelia Rooke (4)
Meadowbrook Primary School, Bradley Stoke

Tily-Lou's First Riddle

What could it be?
Follow the clues and see.

It looks like **a pony**.
It sounds like **a horse**.
It smells like **sugar**.
It feels like **velvet**.
It tastes like **sweets**.

Have you guessed what it could be?
Look below and you will see,
It is...

Answer: A unicorn.

Tily-Lou Tapper (5)
Meadowbrook Primary School, Bradley Stoke

Elise's First Riddle

What could it be?
Follow the clues and see.

It looks like **a mirror**.
It sounds like *splash!*
It smells like **ice**.
It feels like **liquid**.
It tastes **cold**.

Have you guessed what it could be?
Look below and you will see,
It is...

Answer: *Water.*

Elise Hanson (4)
Meadowbrook Primary School, Bradley Stoke

Kaira's First Riddle

What could it be?
Follow the clues and see.

It looks like **snow**.
It sounds like **a horse**.
It smells **sweet**.
It feels like **fur**.
It tastes like **sweets**.

Have you guessed what it could be?
Look below and you will see,
It is...

Answer: A unicorn.

Kaira Kandagatla (4)
Meadowbrook Primary School, Bradley Stoke

Nitya's First Riddle

What could it be?
Follow the clues and see.

It looks like **yellow pearls**.
It sounds **crunchy**.
It smells **fresh**.
It feels like **beads**.
It tastes **sweet**.

Have you guessed what it could be?
Look below and you will see,
It is...

Answer: Corn.

Nitya Agrawal (4)
Meadowbrook Primary School, Bradley Stoke

Layton's First Riddle

What could it be?
Follow the clues and see.

It looks **flat**.
It sounds like **stories**.
It smells like **a library**.
It tastes like **paper**.

Have you guessed what it could be?
Look below and you will see,
It is...

Answer: A book.

Layton Hill (5)
Meadowbrook Primary School, Bradley Stoke

Lyla's First Riddle

What could it be?
Follow the clues and see.

It looks **colourful**.
It sounds like *roar!*
It smells like **cake**.
It feels **lovely**.
It tastes like **cake**.

Have you guessed what it could be?
Look below and you will see,
It is...

Answer: A dragon parade.

Lyla Owen (4)
Meadvale Community Primary School, Worle

Thomas' First Riddle

What could they be?
Follow the clues and see.

They look **curved**.
They sound like *crack!*
They smell like **chicken**.
They feel **smooth**.
They taste like **prawns**.

Have you guessed what they could be?
Look below and you will see,
They are...

Answer: *Prawn crackers.*

Thomas Peter Dunstone (4)
Meadvale Community Primary School, Worle

Ruby's First Riddle

What could it be?
Follow the clues and see.

It looks **yellow**.
It sounds like *slurp!*
It smells like **chicken**.
It feels like **spaghetti**.
It tastes like **chicken**.

Have you guessed what it could be?
Look below and you will see,
It is...

Answer: Noodles.

Ruby Brook (4)
Meadvale Community Primary School, Worle

Kyron's First Riddle

What could it be?
Follow the clues and see.

It looks **red**.
It sounds like *roar!*
It smells like **fire**.
It feels **hot**.
It tastes like **smoke**.

Have you guessed what it could be?
Look below and you will see,
It is...

Answer: A dragon.

Kyron De-Laune (4)
Meadvale Community Primary School, Worle

Charliee's First Riddle

What could it be?
Follow the clues and see.

It looks **red**.
It sounds like *roar!*
It smells like **fire**.
It feels **soft**.
It tastes like **chicken**.

Have you guessed what it could be?
Look below and you will see,
It is...

Answer: A dragon.

Charliee Herring (5)
Meadvale Community Primary School, Worle

Nicky's First Riddle

What could it be?
Follow the clues and see.

It looks like **confetti**.
It sounds like **drums**.
It smells like **fire**.
It feels **soft**.
It tastes like **rice**.

Have you guessed what it could be?
Look below and you will see,
It is...

Answer: A dragon parade.

Nicky Board (5)
Meadvale Community Primary School, Worle

Daphne's First Riddle

What could it be?
Follow the clues and see.

It looks **red**.
It sounds like *roar!*
It smells like **fire**.
It feels **bumpy**.
It tastes **yucky**.

Have you guessed what it could be?
Look below and you will see,
It is...

Answer: A dragon.

Daphne Rose Webster (5)

Meadvale Community Primary School, Worle

Dylan's First Riddle

What could it be?
Follow the clues and see.

It looks **black**.
It sounds like *pop*!
It smells like **Coke**.
It feels like **lemonade**.
It tastes like **fizz**.

Have you guessed what it could be?
Look below and you will see,
It is...

Answer: Cola.

Dylan Burland (4)
Meadvale Community Primary School, Worle

Isaac's First Riddle

What could it be?
Follow the clues and see.

It looks **long**.
It sounds like *slurp!*
It smells **yummy**.
It feels **soft**.
It tastes like **noodles**.

Have you guessed what it could be?
Look below and you will see,
It is...

Answer: Noodles.

Isaac Taylor (5)
Meadvale Community Primary School, Worle

Marco's First Riddle

What could they be?
Follow the clues and see.

They look like **a big display**.
They sound like *boom*!
They smell like **gas**.
They feel like **fire**.

Have you guessed what they could be?
Look below and you will see,
They are...

Answer: Fireworks.

Marco Sutak (5)
Meadvale Community Primary School, Worle

Noah's First Riddle

What could they be?
Follow the clues and see.

They look **pretty**.
They sound like *bang!*
They smell like **smoke**.
They feel like **fire**.

Have you guessed what they could be?
Look below and you will see,
They are...

Answer: Fireworks.

Noah Relton Pow (5)
Meadvale Community Primary School, Worle

Freya's First Riddle

What could they be?
Follow the clues and see.

They look like **sparkles**.
They sound like *bang!*
They smell like **gas**.
They feel **loud**.

Have you guessed what they could be?
Look below and you will see,
They are...

Answer: *Fireworks*.

Freya Roseanne Rogers (5)
Meadvale Community Primary School, Worle

Isla's First Riddle

What could it be?
Follow the clues and see.

It looks **scary**.
It sounds **loud**.
It smells like **smoke**.
It feels **hard**.
It tastes like **blood**.

Have you guessed what it could be?
Look below and you will see,
It is...

Answer: A dragon.

Isla Johnson (5)
Meadvale Community Primary School, Worle

Kai's First Riddle

What could they be?
Follow the clues and see.

They look like **sparkles**.
They sound like *boom*!
They smell like **smoke**.
They feel like **fire**.

Have you guessed what they could be?
Look below and you will see,
They are...

Answer: Fireworks.

Kai Manders (4)
Meadvale Community Primary School, Worle

Riley's First Riddle

What could it be?
Follow the clues and see.

It looks **red**.
It sounds like *pop*!
It smells **fizzy**.
It feels **soggy**.
It tastes **sour**.

Have you guessed what it could be?
Look below and you will see,
It is...

Answer: Cola.

Riley Wyatt (5)
Meadvale Community Primary School, Worle

Layla's First Riddle

What could it be?
Follow the clues and see.

It looks **beautiful**.
It sounds **noisy**.
It smells **nice**.
It feels **soft**.
It tastes **yucky**.

Have you guessed what it could be?
Look below and you will see,
It is...

Answer: A flower.

Layla Poppy Anne Weston (5)
Meadvale Community Primary School, Worle

Max's First Riddle

What could it be?
Follow the clues and see.

It looks **black**.
It sounds like **bubbles**.
It smells **fizzy**.
It feels **cold**.
It tastes **yummy**.

Have you guessed what it could be?
Look below and you will see,
It is...

Answer: Cola.

Max Brimson (4)
Meadvale Community Primary School, Worle

Rocky's First Riddle

What could they be?
Follow the clues and see.

They look like **lights**.
They sound like **pop**.
They smell like **gas**.
They feel like **fire**.

Have you guessed what they could be?
Look below and you will see,
They are...

Answer: Fireworks.

Rocky Thomson (4)
Meadvale Community Primary School, Worle

Oliver's First Riddle

What could they be?
Follow the clues and see.

They look **pretty**.
They sound like **bang**.
They smell like **gas**.
They feel like **fire**.

Have you guessed what they could be?
Look below and you will see,
They are...

Answer: *Fireworks.*

Oliver Booth-Gray (5)
Meadvale Community Primary School, Worle

Samuel's First Riddle

What could it be?
Follow the clues and see.

It looks **long**.
It sounds like **suck**!
It feels **soft**.
It tastes like **chicken**.

Have you guessed what it could be?
Look below and you will see,
It is...

Answer: *Noodles*.

Samuel Morris (5)
Meadvale Community Primary School, Worle

Ruby's First Riddle

What could it be?
Follow the clues and see.

It looks **pretty**.
It sounds like **drums**.
It smells like **rice**.

Have you guessed what it could be?
Look below and you will see,
It is...

Answer: A dragon parade.

Ruby Loretta Young (4)
Meadvale Community Primary School, Worle

Amy's First Riddle

This is my riddle about an amazing animal.
What could it be?
Follow the clues to see!

This animal has **stripes** on its body,
And its colour is **black and white**.
This animal has **four** feet.
It likes **leaves** to eat.
Africa is where it lives.
Its favourite thing to do is **to gallop**.
The animal has **two** ears.
It makes **no** sounds for you to hear.

Are you an animal whizz?
Have you guessed what it is?
It is...

Answer: A zebra.

Amy Morgan (4)
St John's Mead CE (VC) Primary School, Chipping Sodbury

Faith's First Riddle

This is my riddle about an amazing animal.
What could it be?
Follow the clues to see!

This animal has **stripes** on its body,
And its colours are **black and white**.
This animal has **four** feet,
It likes **meat** to eat.
The zoo is where it lives,
Its favourite thing to do is **run,**
This animal has **two** ears,
It makes **a zebra** sound for you to hear.

Are you an animal whizz?
Have you guessed what it is?
It is...

Answer: A zebra.

Faith Louise Holcombe (4)
St John's Mead CE (VC) Primary School, Chipping Sodbury

Sam's First Riddle

This is my riddle about an amazing animal.
What could it be?
Follow the clues to see!

This animal has **black fur** on its body,
And its colour is **black**.
This animal has **hands and feet**,
It likes **meat** to eat.
In a rainforest is where it lives,
Its favourite thing to do is **hit its belly**.
This animal has **two** ears,
It makes **loud** sounds for you to hear.

Are you an animal whizz?
Have you guessed what it is?
It is...

Answer: A gorilla.

Sam Williams (5)
St John's Mead CE (VC) Primary School, Chipping Sodbury

Emily's First Riddle

This is my riddle about an amazing animal.
What could it be?
Follow the clues to see!

This animal has **stripes** on its body,
And its colours are **black and orange**.
This animal has **four** feet,
It likes **meat** to eat.
In the jungle is where it lives,
Its favourite thing to do is **hunt**.
This animal has **two** ears,
It makes **roaring** sounds for you to hear.

Are you an animal whizz?
Have you guessed what it is?
It is...

Answer: A tiger.

Emily Dyson (5)

St John's Mead CE (VC) Primary School, Chipping Sodbury

Ellis' First Riddle

This is my riddle about an amazing animal.
What could it be?
Follow the clues to see!

This animal has **spikes** on its body,
And its colour is **blue**.
This animal has **fourteen** feet,
It likes **cheese** to eat.
On the moon is where it lives,
Its favourite thing to do is **sleep**.
This animal has **no** ears,
It makes **blee-bloo** sounds for you to hear.

Are you an animal whizz?
Have you guessed what it is?
It is...

Answer: An alien.

Ellis Marks (4)
St John's Mead CE (VC) Primary School, Chipping Sodbury

Jess' First Riddle

This is my riddle about an amazing animal.
What could it be?
Follow the clues to see!

This animal has **hair** on its body,
And its colour is **pink sparkles**.
This animal has **four** feet,
It likes **grass** to eat.
On a cloud is where it lives,
Its favourite thing to do is **fly**.
This animal has **two** ears,
It makes **magical** sounds for you to hear.

Are you an animal whizz?
Have you guessed what it is?
It is...

Answer: A unicorn.

Jess Maillardet (5)
St John's Mead CE (VC) Primary School, Chipping Sodbury

Sofia's First Riddle

This is my riddle about an amazing animal.
What could it be?
Follow the clues to see!

This animal has **fur** on its body,
And its colour is **black**.
This animal has **two big** feet,
It likes **grass** to eat.
A jungle is where it lives,
Its favourite thing to do is **swing in trees**.
This animal has **two** ears,
It makes **loud** sounds for you to hear.

Are you an animal whizz?
Have you guessed what it is?
It is...

Answer: A gorilla.

Sofia Curtis-Whitfield (4)
St John's Mead CE (VC) Primary School, Chipping
Sodbury

Bronte's First Riddle

This is my riddle about an amazing animal.
What could it be?
Follow the clues to see!

This animal has **fur** on its body,
And its colour is **golden**.
This animal has **four** feet,
It likes **bones** to eat.
At the vet's is where it lives,
Its favourite thing to do is **play**.
This animal has **long** ears,
It makes **barking** sounds for you to hear.

Are you an animal whizz?
Have you guessed what it is?
It is...

Answer: A puppy.

Bronte Coleman (4)
St John's Mead CE (VC) Primary School, Chipping Sodbury

Winter's First Riddle

This is my riddle about an amazing animal.
What could it be?
Follow the clues to see!

This animal has **hair** on its body,
And its colour is **brown**.
This animal has **four** feet,
It likes **carrots** to eat.
In a stable is where it lives,
Its favourite thing to do is **run around**.
This animal has **two** ears,
It makes **neigh** sounds for you to hear.

Are you an animal whizz?
Have you guessed what it is?
It is...

Answer: A horse.

Winter Clarke (5)
St John's Mead CE (VC) Primary School, Chipping Sodbury

Mia's First Riddle

This is my riddle about an amazing animal.
What could it be?
Follow the clues to see!

This animal has **spots** on its body,
And its colour is **yellow**.
This animal has **long** feet,
It likes **leaves** to eat.
In the zoo is where it lives,
Its favourite thing to do is **lick**.
This animal has **pretty** ears,
It makes **funny** sounds for you to hear.

Are you an animal whizz?
Have you guessed what it is?
It is...

Answer: A *giraffe*.

Mia Prosser (5)
St John's Mead CE (VC) Primary School, Chipping Sodbury

Charlie's First Riddle

This is my riddle about an amazing animal.
What could it be?
Follow the clues to see!

This animal has **feathers** on its body,
And its colour is **yellow**.
This animal has **two** feet,
It likes **worms** to eat.
A bird cage is where it lives,
Its favourite thing to do is **fly**.
This animal has **two** ears,
It makes **chirpy** sounds for you to hear.

Are you an animal whizz?
Have you guessed what it is?
It is...

Answer: A canary.

Charlie Townsend (5)
St John's Mead CE (VC) Primary School, Chipping Sodbury

Henry's First Riddle

This is my riddle about an amazing animal.
What could it be?
Follow the clues to see!

This animal has **spikes** on its body,
And its colour is **green**.
This animal has **four** feet,
It likes **fish** to eat.
A swamp is where it lives,
Its favourite thing to do is **swim**.
This animal has **two** ears,
It makes **snapping** sounds for you to hear.

Are you an animal whizz?
Have you guessed what it is?
It is...

Answer: A crocodile.

Henry McMeechan (4)
St John's Mead CE (VC) Primary School, Chipping Sodbury

Emily's First Riddle

This is my riddle about an amazing animal.
What could it be?
Follow the clues to see!

This animal has **fur** on its body,
And its colour is **white**.
This animal has **four** feet,
It likes **fish** to eat.
An island is where it lives,
Its favourite thing to do is **sleep**.
This animal has **two** ears,
It makes **roaring** sounds for you to hear.

Are you an animal whizz?
Have you guessed what it is?
It is...

Answer: A polar bear.

Emily Humphreys (4)
St John's Mead CE (VC) Primary School, Chipping Sodbury

Nia's First Riddle

This is my riddle about an amazing animal.
What could it be?
Follow the clues to see!

This animal has **feathers** on its body,
And its colour is **black**.
This animal has **two** feet,
It likes **worms** to eat.
A tree is where it lives,
Its favourite thing to do is **fly**.
This animal has **two** ears,
It makes **squawking** sounds for you to hear.

Are you an animal whizz?
Have you guessed what it is?
It is...

Answer: A seagull.

Nia Morgan (5)
St John's Mead CE (VC) Primary School, Chipping Sodbury

54

James' First Riddle

This is my riddle about an amazing animal.
What could it be?
Follow the clues to see!

This animal has **grey skin** on its body,
And its colour is **grey**.
This animal has **no** feet,
It likes **fish** to eat.
The sea is where it lives,
Its favourite thing to do is **hunt**.
This animal has **two** ears,
It makes **snap, snap** sounds for you to hear.

Are you an animal whizz?
Have you guessed what it is?
It is...

Answer: A shark.

James Ian John Taylor (5)
St John's Mead CE (VC) Primary School, Chipping
Sodbury

Jacob's First Riddle

This is my riddle about an amazing animal.
What could it be?
Follow the clues to see!

This animal has **skin** on its body,
And its colour is **pink**.
This animal has **four** feet,
It likes **carrots** to eat.
A farm is where it lives,
Its favourite thing to do is **roll in mud**.
This animal has **two** ears,
It makes **oink** sounds for you to hear.

Are you an animal whizz?
Have you guessed what it is?
It is...

Answer: A pig.

Jacob Whittingham (5)
St John's Mead CE (VC) Primary School, Chipping Sodbury

Imogen's First Riddle

This is my riddle about an amazing animal.
What could it be?
Follow the clues to see!

This animal has **fur** on its body,
And its colour is **brown**.
This animal has **four** feet,
It likes **bananas** to eat.
A jungle is where it lives,
Its favourite thing to do is **swing**.
This animal has **two** ears,
It makes **aaah** sounds for you to hear.

Are you an animal whizz?
Have you guessed what it is?
It is...

Answer: A monkey.

Imogen Chloe Allen (5)
St John's Mead CE (VC) Primary School, Chipping
Sodbury

Kelsey's First Riddle

This is my riddle about an amazing animal.
What could it be?
Follow the clues to see!

This animal has **fur** on its body,
And its colour is **pink**.
This animal has **four** feet,
It likes **grass** to eat.
In the jungle is where it lives,
Its favourite thing to do is **eat**.
This animal has **two** ears,
It makes **big** sounds for you to hear.

Are you an animal whizz?
Have you guessed what it is?
It is...

Answer: A unicorn.

Kelsey Hewitt (4)
St John's Mead CE (VC) Primary School, Chipping Sodbury

Oscar's First Riddle

This is my riddle about an amazing animal.
What could it be?
Follow the clues to see!

This animal has **fur** on its body,
And its colour is **black**.
This animal has **four** feet,
It likes **ham** to eat.
A house is where it lives,
Its favourite thing to do is **sleep**.
This animal has **two** ears,
It makes **meow** sounds for you to hear.

Are you an animal whizz?
Have you guessed what it is?
It is...

Answer: A cat.

Oscar Robert Batten (4)
St John's Mead CE (VC) Primary School, Chipping Sodbury

Braxton's First Riddle

This is my riddle about an amazing animal.
What could it be?
Follow the clues to see!

This animal has **feathers** on its body,
And its colours are **black and white**.
This animal has **two** feet,
It likes **fish** to eat.
The North Pole is where it lives.
This animal has **two** ears,
It makes **noisy** sounds for you to hear.

Are you an animal whizz?
Have you guessed what it is?
It is...

Answer: A penguin.

Braxton Watmough (4)
St John's Mead CE (VC) Primary School, Chipping Sodbury

Sophia's First Riddle

This is my riddle about an amazing animal.
What could it be?
Follow the clues to see!

This animal has **spots** on its body,
And its colour is **yellow**.
This animal has **two** feet,
It likes **trees** to eat.
In the jungle is where it lives,
Its favourite thing to do is **eat**.
This animal has **two** ears.

Are you an animal whizz?
Have you guessed what it is?
It is...

Answer: A giraffe.

Sophia Morgan (4)
St John's Mead CE (VC) Primary School, Chipping Sodbury

Lottie's First Riddle

This is my riddle about an amazing animal.
What could it be?
Follow the clues to see!

This animal has **pink** on its body.
This animal has **two** feet,
It likes **fish** to eat.
Africa is where it lives,
Its favourite thing to do is **stand**.
This animal has **two** ears.

Are you an animal whizz?
Have you guessed what it is?
It is...

Answer: A flamingo.

Lottie Carpenter (4)
St John's Mead CE (VC) Primary School, Chipping Sodbury

Esmae's First Riddle

This is my riddle about an amazing animal.
What could it be?
Follow the clues to see!

This animal has **fur** on its body,
And its colour is **black**.
This animal has **four** feet,
It likes **ham** to eat.
In a house is where it lives,
Its favourite thing to do is **sleep**.

Are you an animal whizz?
Have you guessed what it is?
It is...

Answer: A cat.

Esmae Williams-Dracup (4)
St John's Mead CE (VC) Primary School, Chipping Sodbury

Imogen's First Riddle

This is my riddle about an amazing animal.
What could it be?
Follow the clues to see!

This animal has **hair** on its body,
And its colour is **white**.
This animal has **four** feet,
It likes **food** to eat.
Daisy's house is where it lives,
Its favourite thing to do is **bite**.
This animal has **two** ears,
It makes **meow** sounds for you to hear.

Are you an animal whizz?
Have you guessed what it is?
It is...

Answer: A cat.

Imogen Sophie Holland (4)
St Mary's CE Primary School, Timsbury

Joshua's First Riddle

This is my riddle about an amazing animal.
What could it be?
Follow the clues to see!

This animal has **spots** on its body,
And its colour is **yellow**.
This animal has **four** feet,
It likes **leaves** to eat.
The zoo is where it lives,
Its favourite thing to do is **grab leaves**.
This animal has **two** ears,
It makes **no** sounds for you to hear.

Are you an animal whizz?
Have you guessed what it is?
It is...

Answer: A giraffe.

Joshua Wills (4)
St Mary's CE Primary School, Timsbury

Daisy's First Riddle

This is my riddle about an amazing animal.
What could it be?
Follow the clues to see!

This animal has **fur** on its body,
And its colour is **white**.
This animal has **four** feet,
It likes **carrots** to eat.
On a rainbow is where it lives,
Its favourite thing to do is **fly**.
This animal has **two** ears,
It makes **neigh** sounds for you to hear.

Are you an animal whizz?
Have you guessed what it is?
It is...

Answer: A unicorn.

Daisy Miell (4)
St Mary's CE Primary School, Timsbury

Jenson's First Riddle

This is my riddle about an amazing animal.
What could it be?
Follow the clues to see!

This animal has **a fin** on its body,
And its colour is **grey**.
This animal has **no** feet,
It likes **fish** to eat.
The sea is where it lives,
Its favourite thing to do is **swim**.
This animal has **no** ears,
It makes **no** sounds for you to hear.

Are you an animal whizz?
Have you guessed what it is?
It is...

Answer: A shark.

Jenson Squire (5)
St Mary's CE Primary School, Timsbury

Finley's First Riddle

This is my riddle about an amazing animal.
What could it be?
Follow the clues to see!

This animal has **fins** on its body,
And its colour is **light grey**.
This animal has **no** feet,
It likes **fish** to eat.
In water is where it lives,
Its favourite thing to do is **play**.
This animal has **no** ears.

Are you an animal whizz?
Have you guessed what it is?
It is...

Answer: A dolphin.

Finley Josh Humphries (5)
St Mary's CE Primary School, Timsbury

Toby's First Riddle

What could it be?
Follow the clues and see.

It looks **orange and black**.
It sounds like *roar!*
It smells like **meat and fish**.
It feels **bumpy**.
It tastes like **a chocolate orange**.

Have you guessed what it could be?
Look below and you will see,
It is...

Answer: A tiger.

Toby Blake (5)
St Mary's CE Primary School, Yate

Cassie's First Riddle

What could it be?
Follow the clues and see.

It looks **stripy**.
It sounds like *clippity-clop!*
It smells like **sand**.
It feels like **fur**.
It tastes like **paper**.

Have you guessed what it could be?
Look below and you will see,
It is...

Answer: A zebra.

Cassie Grier (5)
St Mary's CE Primary School, Yate

Emelia's First Riddle

What could it be?
Follow the clues and see.

It looks **brown, white and black.**
It sounds like *woof, woof!*
It smells like **bones.**
It feels **soft and fluffy.**
It tastes like **chocolate.**

Have you guessed what it could be?
Look below and you will see,
It is...

Answer: A dog.

Emelia Welsford (5)
St Mary's CE Primary School, Yate

Jonah's First Riddle

What could it be?
Follow the clues and see.

It looks like **a tree**.
It sounds like *roar!*
It smells like **stinky rubbish**.
It feels **bumpy**.
It tastes like **roast beef**.

Have you guessed what it could be?
Look below and you will see,
It is...

Answer: A dinosaur.

Jonah Harris (4)
St Mary's CE Primary School, Yate

Eddie's First Riddle

What could it be?
Follow the clues and see.

It looks like **bumpy skin.**
It sounds like *snap, snap!*
It smells like **dirt.**
It feels **hard.**
It tastes **not very nice.**

Have you guessed what it could be?
Look below and you will see,
It is...

Answer: A crocodile.

Eddie Fitton (4)
St Mary's CE Primary School, Yate

Alfie's First Riddle

What could it be?
Follow the clues and see.

It looks **green**.
It sounds like *snap, snap!*
It smells like **smelly water**.
It feels **bumpy**.
It tastes like **seaweed**.

Have you guessed what it could be?
Look below and you will see,
It is...

Answer: A crocodile.

Alfie Pearce (5)
St Mary's CE Primary School, Yate

Robyn's First Riddle

What could it be?
Follow the clues and see.

It looks **brown and hairy.**
It sounds like **an elephant.**
It smells like **flowers.**
It feels like **Daddy's hair.**
It tastes like **meat.**

Have you guessed what it could be?
Look below and you will see,
It is...

Answer: A woolly mammoth.

Robyn Ellen Gapper (5)
St Mary's CE Primary School, Yate

Archie's First Riddle

What could it be?
Follow the clues and see.

It has **two wings**.
It sounds like *tweet tweet!*
It smells like **a tree**.
It feels **soft**.
It tastes like **yucky tickly feathers**.

Have you guessed what it could be?
Look below and you will see,
It is...

Answer: A bird.

Archie Jones (4)
St Mary's CE Primary School, Yate

Zac's First Riddle

What could it be?
Follow the clues and see.

It looks like **a spotty cheetah**.
It sounds like **a *slurp*!**
It smells **very lovely**.
It feels **hard**.
It tastes like **beef**.

Have you guessed what it could be?
Look below and you will see,
It is...

Answer: A giraffe.

Zac De Nobriga (4)
St Mary's CE Primary School, Yate

Adalae's First Riddle

What could it be?
Follow the clues and see.

It looks like **brown fur**.
It sounds like *woof, woof*!
It smells like **shampoo**.
It feels **fluffy**.
It tastes like **sausages**.

Have you guessed what it could be?
Look below and you will see,
It is...

Answer: A dog.

Adalae Smith (5)
St Mary's CE Primary School, Yate

Mia's First Riddle

What could it be?
Follow the clues and see.

It looks like **the sunrise**.
It sounds like **nothing**.
It smells like **a juicy strawberry**.
It feels **smooth**.
It tastes like **cinnamon**.

Have you guessed what it could be?
Look below and you will see,
It is...

Answer: A flower.

Mia Jane Wiltshire (5)
St Mary's CE Primary School, Yate

Samuel's First Riddle

What could it be?
Follow the clues and see.

It looks like **sharp teeth**.
It sounds like *roar!*
It smells **stinky**.
It feels like **bumpy stones**.
It tastes like **meat**.

Have you guessed what it could be?
Look below and you will see,
It is...

Answer: A *T-rex*.

Samuel Shipp (5)
St Mary's CE Primary School, Yate

Sienna's First Riddle

What could it be?
Follow the clues and see.

It looks like **fluffy wool**.
It sounds like *baa*!
It smells like **dirty mud**.
It feels like **soft wool**.
It tastes like **a banana**.

Have you guessed what it could be?
Look below and you will see,
It is...

Answer: A sheep.

Sienna Hollister-Rushent (5)
St Mary's CE Primary School, Yate

Cali's First Riddle

What could it be?
Follow the clues and see.

It looks like **a rectangle**.
It sounds **crunchy**.
It smells like **a strawberry**.
It feels **hard**.
It tastes **delicious**.

Have you guessed what it could be?
Look below and you will see,
It is...

Answer: Chocolate.

Cali Jefferies (4)
St Mary's CE Primary School, Yate

Maisie's First Riddle

What could it be?
Follow the clues and see.

It looks like **a lion**.
It sounds like *woof!*
It smells like **biscuits**.
It feels **hairy and soft**.
It tastes like **yucky mud**.

Have you guessed what it could be?
Look below and you will see,
It is...

Answer: A dog.

Maisie Leach (4)
St Mary's CE Primary School, Yate

Mollie's First Riddle

What could it be?
Follow the clues and see.

It looks like **a person**.
It sounds **crunchy**.
It smells like **lovely ginger**.
It feels **hard**.
It tastes **tasty and yummy**.

Have you guessed what it could be?
Look below and you will see,
It is...

Answer: A gingerbread man.

Mollie Matten (5)
St Mary's CE Primary School, Yate

Charlie's First Riddle

What could it be?
Follow the clues and see.

It looks **furry**.
It sounds like **merr**!
It smells like **hay**.
It feels **very soft**.
It tastes like **chocolate**.

Have you guessed what it could be?
Look below and you will see,
It is...

Answer: A goat.

Charlie Sivell (4)
St Mary's CE Primary School, Yate

Tayton's First Riddle

What could it be?
Follow the clues and see.

It looks like **a red nose**.
It sounds **squidgy**.
It smells like **cherries**.
It feels **smooth**.
It tastes **wet and juicy**.

Have you guessed what it could be?
Look below and you will see,
It is...

Answer: A strawberry.

Tayton Andrews (4)
St Mary's CE Primary School, Yate

Elizabeth's First Riddle

What could it be?
Follow the clues and see.

It has **a furry tail**.
It sounds like **woof, woof**!
It smells like **dirt**.
It feels **soft**.
It tastes **chewy**.

Have you guessed what it could be?
Look below and you will see,
It is...

Answer: A dog.

Elizabeth Bird (4)
St Mary's CE Primary School, Yate

Mason-Lee's First Riddle

What could it be?
Follow the clues and see.

It looks **black and brown**.
It sounds like *neigh!*
It smells like **grass**.
It feels **soft**.
It tastes like **grass**.

Have you guessed what it could be?
Look below and you will see,
It is...

Answer: A horse.

Mason-Lee Cahill (4)
St Mary's CE Primary School, Yate

Jack's First Riddle

What could it be?
Follow the clues and see.

It looks **white**.
It sounds **crunchy**.
It smells like **a strawberry**.
It feels like **it is hard**.
It tastes **yummy**.

Have you guessed what it could be?
Look below and you will see,
It is...

Answer: A chocolate bar.

Jack Sady (5)
St Mary's CE Primary School, Yate

Finley's First Riddle

What could it be?
Follow the clues and see.

It looks like **a dinosaur**.
It sounds like **neigh**.
It smells like **hay**.
It feels **fluffy**.
It tastes like **chocolate**.

Have you guessed what it could be?
Look below and you will see,
It is...

Answer: A horse.

Finley Thomas (5)
St Mary's CE Primary School, Yate

Ella's First Riddle

What could it be?
Follow the clues and see.

It looks **brown**.
It sounds like **merr**!
It smells like **hay**.
It feels **fluffy**.
It tastes **yucky**.

Have you guessed what it could be?
Look below and you will see,
It is...

Answer: A goat.

Ella Grace Stone (4)
St Mary's CE Primary School, Yate

Erin's First Riddle

What could it be?
Follow the clues and see.

It looks like **a rectangle**.
It sounds like **a mouse**.
It smells like **cake**.
It feels **hard**.
It tastes **yummy**.

Have you guessed what it could be?
Look below and you will see,
It is...

Answer: Chocolate.

Erin Bartlett (4)
St Mary's CE Primary School, Yate

Max's First Riddle

What could it be?
Follow the clues and see.

It has **two horns**.
It sounds like *moo!*
It smells like **grass**.
It feels **smooth**.
It tastes like **fur**.

Have you guessed what it could be?
Look below and you will see,
It is...

Answer: A bull.

Max Rivett (5)
St Mary's CE Primary School, Yate

Rosa's First Riddle

What could it be?
Follow the clues and see.

It looks like **a long tail**.
It sounds like **eating**.
It smells like **sand**.
It feels **soft**.
It tastes **yum**.

Have you guessed what it could be?
Look below and you will see,
It is...

Answer: A kangaroo.

Rosa Ellen Base (4)
St Mary's CE Primary School, Yate

Phoebe's First Riddle

What could it be?
Follow the clues and see.

It has **a long tail**.
It sounds like **a lion**.
It smells like **flowers**.
It feels **hard**.
It tastes **chewy**.

Have you guessed what it could be?
Look below and you will see,
It is...

Answer: A dinosaur.

Phoebe Miles (4)
St Mary's CE Primary School, Yate

Olivia's First Riddle

What could it be?
Follow the clues and see.

It looks like **sand.**
It sounds like *crunch!*
It smells **yummy.**
It feels **hard.**
It tastes **nice.**

Have you guessed what it could be?
Look below and you will see,
It is...

Answer: A cookie.

Olivia Everson (5)
St Mary's CE Primary School, Yate

Elizabeth's First Riddle

What could it be?
Follow the clues and see.

It looks like **a big nose**.
It smells like **sweets**.
It feels like **water**.
It tastes like **juice from an apple**.

Have you guessed what it could be?
Look below and you will see,
It is...

Answer: A strawberry.

Elizabeth Gay (4)
St Mary's CE Primary School, Yate

Hattie's First Riddle

What could it be?
Follow the clues and see.

It looks like **a fairy house**.
It smells like **mud**.
It feels like **a soft dog**.
It tastes like **yummy children**.

Have you guessed what it could be?
Look below and you will see,
It is...

Answer: A mushroom.

Hattie Wilburn (4)

St Mary's CE Primary School, Yate

Isaac's First Riddle

Who could it be?
Follow the clues and see.

He looks like **a blue coat**.
He sounds like **a knock on the door**.
He smells like **material**.
He feels **soft**.

Have you guessed who he could be?
Look below and you will see,
He is...

Answer: Postman Pat.

Isaac Blacket (5)
St Mary's CE Primary School, Yate

George's First Riddle

Who could it be?
Follow the clues and see.

He looks like **a blue coat**.
He sounds **happy**.
He smells like **a shop**.
He feels **soft**.

Have you guessed who he could be?
Look below and you will see,
He is...

Answer: **Postman Pat**.

George Jago (5)
St Mary's CE Primary School, Yate

Isabel's First Riddle

What could it be?
Follow the clues and see.

It looks like **tall, long legs**.
It sounds like **a loud neigh**.
It smells like **shampoo**.
It feels like **a soft brush**.
It tastes like **muffins (its name)**.

Have you guessed what it could be?
Look below and you will see,
It is...

Answer: A horse.

Isabel Basson (4)
St Nicholas CE Primary School, Henstridge

Isaac's First Riddle

What could it be?
Follow the clues and see.

It looks like **brown water**.
It sounds like *glug!*
It smells like **chocolate cake**.
It feels like **a kettle**.
It tastes like **milk**.

Have you guessed what it could be?
Look below and you will see,
It is...

Answer: Chocolate milk.

Isaac George New (4)
St Nicholas CE Primary School, Henstridge

My First Riddle

What could it be?
Follow the clues and see.

It looks like **a red ball**.
It sounds like *splat*!
It smells like **sweet juice**.
It feels **squidgy**.
It tastes like **a yummy explosion**.

Have you guessed what it could be?
Look below and you will see,
It is...

Answer: A tomato.

E Hancock (4)
St Nicholas CE Primary School, Henstridge

Maddison's First Riddle

What could it be?
Follow the clues and see.

It looks like **a spiky ball**.
It sounds like **noisy squeaks**.
It smells like **cat food**.
It feels like **prickles**.
It tastes like **nothing**.

Have you guessed what it could be?
Look below and you will see,
It is...

Answer: A hedgehog.

Maddison Elliott (4)
St Nicholas CE Primary School, Henstridge

Logan's First Riddle

What could it be?
Follow the clues and see.

It looks like **brown stuff**.
It sounds like *glug!*
It smells like **chocolate**.
It feels like **cola**.
It tastes **yummy**.

Have you guessed what it could be?
Look below and you will see,
It is...

Answer: Ice cream.

Logan Sunley (5)
St Nicholas CE Primary School, Henstridge

McKenzie's First Riddle

What could it be?
Follow the clues and see.

It looks like **a white cloud**.
It sounds like **a soft wind**.
It smells like **snow**.
It feels **crunchy**.
It tastes like **water**.

Have you guessed what it could be?
Look below and you will see,
It is...

Answer: A snowman.

McKenzie Murphy (4)
St Nicholas CE Primary School, Henstridge

Jake's First Riddle

What could it be?
Follow the clues and see.

It looks like **a round planet**.
It sounds like **nothing**.
It smells like **wet tears**.
It feels **slimy**.
It tastes **horrible**.

Have you guessed what it could be?
Look below and you will see,
It is...

Answer: *An eyeball.*

Jake Stanley (5)
St Nicholas CE Primary School, Henstridge

Kaydee-Leigh's First Riddle

What could it be?
Follow the clues and see.

It looks like **fat circle**.
It sounds like *crack!*
It smells **strong**.
It feels **slimy**.
It tastes **yummy**.

Have you guessed what it could be?
Look below and you will see,
It is...

Answer: An egg.

Kaydee-Leigh Amelie Downton (5)
St Nicholas CE Primary School, Henstridge

Grace's First Riddle

What could it be?
Follow the clues and see.

It looks like **a fur ball**.
It sounds like **a squeak**.
It smells like **hay**.
It feels like **soft wool**.
It tastes **chewy**.

Have you guessed what it could be?
Look below and you will see,
It is...

Answer: A mouse.

Grace Windsor (5)
St Nicholas CE Primary School, Henstridge

Archie's First Riddle

What could it be?
Follow the clues and see.

It looks like **a red circle**.
It sounds **crunchy**.
It smells like **good food**.
It feels **cold**.
It tastes like **sweets**.

Have you guessed what it could be?
Look below and you will see,
It is...

Answer: An apple.

Archie Parsons (4)
St Nicholas CE Primary School, Henstridge

110

Alfie's First Riddle

What could it be?
Follow the clues and see.

It looks like **a hard shell**.
It sounds **slidy**.
It smells like **mud**.
It feels like **slime**.
It tastes like **dirt**.

Have you guessed what it could be?
Look below and you will see,
It is...

Answer: A snail.

Alfie McKenna (4)
St Nicholas CE Primary School, Henstridge

Our First Riddle

What could it be?
Follow the clues and see.

It looks like **a snowball and a balloon.**
It sounds like **nothing at all.**
It smells like **bubblegum and sweets.**
It feels like **a bouncy ball.**
It tastes like **chewing gum.**

Have you guessed what it could be?
Look below and you will see,
It is...

Answer: A marshmallow.

Freddie Brown (5), Ada, Violet, Fynn & Henry
Trinity Church Primary School, Radstock

Our First Riddle

What could it be?
Follow the clues and see.

It looks like **snow and cotton balls**.
It sounds **squishy and bubbly**.
It smells like **a cloud**.
It feels **sticky and squishy**.
It tastes **sweet**.

Have you guessed what it could be?
Look below and you will see,
It is...

Answer: A marshmallow.

Jacob Shearn (4), Leo, Tobious Mark Edward Wightman (4) & Aron
Trinity Church Primary School, Radstock

Our First Riddle

What could it be?
Follow the clues and see.

It looks like **a cloud**.
It sounds like **popping**.
It smells like **sweet bubblegum**.
It feels **squishy**.
It tastes like **bubbles**.

Have you guessed what it could be?
Look below and you will see,
It is...

Answer: A marshmallow.

Savannah Evans-Isaac (5), Amber, Alfred R (5), Riley & Orrv
Trinity Church Primary School, Radstock

Victor's First Riddle

What could it be?
Follow the clues and see.

It looks like **a little person**.
It sounds like *crunch crunch*!
It smells like **ginger**.
It feels like **a warm cookie**.
It tastes like **sweet Christmas**.

Have you guessed what it could be?
Look below and you will see,
It is...

Answer: A gingerbread man.

Victor Posea (5)
Wansdyke Primary School, Whitchurch

Joey's First Riddle

What could it be?
Follow the clues and see.

It looks like **red T-shirts, shorts and socks.**
It sounds like **people cheering loudly.**
It smells like **smoke and food.**
It feels like **cold wind on my face.**
It tastes like **nothing.**

Have you guessed what it could be?
Look below and you will see,
It is...

Answer: *Liverpool Football Club.*

Joey Chillcott (4)
Wansdyke Primary School, Whitchurch

Carter's First Riddle

Where could it be?
Follow the clues and see.

It looks like **blue sky and sandy beaches.**
It sounds like **reggae music.**
It smells like **spicy chicken, dumplings and barbecues.**
It feels **very warm.**
It tastes like **spicy food and curry goat.**

Have you guessed where it could be?
Look below and you will see,
It is...

Answer: Jamaica.

Carter Tulloch (4)
Wansdyke Primary School, Whitchurch

Kaiyrian-Jay's First Riddle

Who could it be?
Follow the clues and see.

She looks like **a princess**.
She sounds like **a loud drum**.
She smells like **flowers**.
She feels like **clouds**.
She tastes like **candy**.

Have you guessed who she could be?
Look below and you will see,
She is...

Answer: My mummy.

Kaiyrian-Jay McKenzie West (4)
Wansdyke Primary School, Whitchurch

Albie's First Riddle

Who could it be?
Follow the clues and see.

He looks like **a grandad**.
He sounds like **jingle bells**.
He smells like **soot and coal**.
He feels like **magic**.
He tastes like **cookies and milk**.

Have you guessed who he could be?
Look below and you will see,
He is...

Answer: *Father Christmas!*

Albie White (4)
Wansdyke Primary School, Whitchurch

Renae's First Riddle

What could it be?
Follow the clues and see.

It looks like **green grass**.
It sounds like *roar!*
It smells like **rotten meat**.
It feels **slippery**.
It tastes like **stinky underpants**.

Have you guessed what it could be?
Look below and you will see,
It is...

Answer: A dinosaur.

Renae Coulton (4)
Wansdyke Primary School, Whitchurch

Sienna's First Riddle

What could it be?
Follow the clues and see.

It looks like **an egg**.
It sounds like **wrapping paper**.
It smells like **strawberry**.
It feels like **plastic**.
It tastes like **rubber**.

Have you guessed what it could be?
Look below and you will see,
It is...

Answer: A L.O.L. doll.

Sienna Carnevale (5)
Wansdyke Primary School, Whitchurch

Kai's First Riddle

What could it be?
Follow the clues and see.

It looks like **a little ball**.
It sounds **quiet**.
It smells **fresh**.
It feels **squidgy**.
It tastes **yummy**.

Have you guessed what it could be?
Look below and you will see,
It is...

Answer: A pea.

Kai Saunders (4)
Wansdyke Primary School, Whitchurch

Lily's First Riddle

What could it be?
Follow the clues and see.

It looks **brown, has two legs and two arms**.
It sounds like ***ooo-aaah***!
It smells like **bananas**.
It feels like **compost**.
It tastes like **a banana**.

Have you guessed what it could be?
Look below and you will see,
It is...

Answer: A monkey.

Lily Collins (5)
Westover Green Community School, Westover Green

Lillie's First Riddle

What could it be?
Follow the clues and see.

It looks **black**.
It sounds like *ooo-aah*!
It smells like **apples**.
It feels like **a furry head**.
It tastes like **meat**.

Have you guessed what it could be?
Look below and you will see,
It is...

Answer: A gorilla.

Lillie Pocock (5)
Westover Green Community School, Westover Green

Rebecca's First Riddle

What could it be?
Follow the clues and see.

It looks like **a horse with a horn.**
It sounds like **a horse.**
It smells like **a rainbow.**
It feels like **a rainbow.**
It tastes like **a fairy.**

Have you guessed what it could be?
Look below and you will see,
It is...

Answer: A unicorn.

Rebecca Hook (5)
Westover Green Community School, Westover
Green

Azala's First Riddle

What could it be?
Follow the clues and see.

It looks like **it has wings**.
It sounds like **tweet**!
It smells like **flowers**.
It feels **soft**.
It tastes like **yucky wings**.

Have you guessed what it could be?
Look below and you will see,
It is...

Answer: A bird.

Azala Ashley Baker (4)
Westover Green Community School, Westover Green

Jack's First Riddle

What could it be?
Follow the clues and see.

It looks like **a leopard**.
It sounds like **a race car**.
It smells like **a clean owl**.
It feels like **a cat**.
It tastes like **a furry monkey**.

Have you guessed what it could be?
Look below and you will see,
It is...

Answer: A cheetah.

Jack Stark (4)
Westover Green Community School, Westover
Green

Lucy's First Riddle

What could it be?
Follow the clues and see.

It looks **furry and has pointy ears.**
It sounds like *miaow!*
It smells like **meat.**
It feels **furry.**
It tastes like **cat food.**

Have you guessed what it could be?
Look below and you will see,
It is...

Answer: A cat.

Lucy Lilyrose Newland (5)
Westover Green Community School, Westover Green

Lilly-Rose's First Riddle

What could it be?
Follow the clues and see.

It looks **black and brown**.
It sounds like *woof, woof!*
It smells like **poo**.
It feels **fluffy**.
It tastes like **sausages**.

Have you guessed what it could be?
Look below and you will see,
It is...

ˈƃop ∀ :ɹǝʍsu∀

Lilly-Rose German (4)
Westover Green Community School, Westover Green

YoungWriters Est. 1991

Jordan's First Riddle

What could it be?
Follow the clues and see.

It looks **yellow and orange**.
It sounds like **a dinosaur**.
It smells like **poo**.
It feels **fluffy**.
It tastes **disgusting**.

Have you guessed what it could be?
Look below and you will see,
It is...

Answer: A tiger.

Jordan Davis (5)
Westover Green Community School, Westover
Green

130

Alisha-Marie's First Riddle

What could it be?
Follow the clues and see.

It looks **furry and it has whiskers**.
It sounds like *miaow!*
It smells like **cat food**.
It feels like **fur**.
It tastes like **fish**.

Have you guessed what it could be?
Look below and you will see,
It is...

Answer: A cat.

Alisha-Marie Warren (5)
Westover Green Community School, Westover Green

Jasper's First Riddle

What could it be?
Follow the clues and see.

It looks **big and grey**.
It sounds like **a loud trumpet**.
It smells like **a stinky sock**.
It feels **smooth**.
It tastes like **rubber**.

Have you guessed what it could be?
Look below and you will see,
It is...

Answer: An elephant.

Jasper Brown (4)

Westover Green Community School, Westover Green

Tobie-Jai's First Riddle

What could it be?
Follow the clues and see.

It looks like **wheels**.
It sounds like *vrrrrmm!*
It smells like **petrol**.
It feels **smooth**.
It tastes like **petrol**.

Have you guessed what it could be?
Look below and you will see,
It is...

Answer: A car.

Tobie-Jai Hammett (4)

Westover Green Community School, Westover
Green

Violet's First Riddle

What could it be?
Follow the clues and see.

It looks **stripy**.
It sounds like *roar!*
It smells **disgusting**.
It feels **soft**.
It tastes like **bones**.

Have you guessed what it could be?
Look below and you will see,
It is...

Answer: A tiger.

Violet Brooks (4)
Westover Green Community School, Westover Green

134

Jaylen's First Riddle

What could it be?
Follow the clues and see.

It looks like **a long trunk**.
It sounds like **a trumpet**.
It smells like **mud**.
It feels **smooth**.
It tastes like **a stinky poo**.

Have you guessed what it could be?
Look below and you will see,
It is...

Answer: An elephant.

Jaylen Fursland (4)
Westover Green Community School, Westover
Green

Skajus' First Riddle

What could it be?
Follow the clues and see.

It looks **big**.
It sounds like **eee, eee**!
It smells **good**.
It feels **hairy**.
It tastes like **bananas**.

Have you guessed what it could be?
Look below and you will see,
It is...

Answer: A monkey.

Skajus Rapsevicius (4)
Westover Green Community School, Westover Green

Kiowa's First Riddle

What could it be?
Follow the clues and see.

It looks **grey**.
It sounds like **a trumpet**.
It smells like **a stinky insect**.
It feels **tough**.
It tastes like **mouldy food**.

Have you guessed what it could be?
Look below and you will see,
It is...

Answer: An elephant.

Kiowa Erkhagen (4)
Westover Green Community School, Westover
Green

Archie's First Riddle

What could it be?
Follow the clues and see.

It looks **brown**.
It sounds like *oooh*!
It smells like **a banana**.
It feels like **a rabbit**.
It tastes like **rubbish**.

Have you guessed what it could be?
Look below and you will see,
It is...

Answer: A monkey.

Archie Locke (4)
Westover Green Community School, Westover
Green

Ella's First Riddle

What could it be?
Follow the clues and see.

It looks **brown**.
It sounds like *oooh-oooh*!
It smells like **branches**.
It feels **soft**.
It tastes like **a banana**.

Have you guessed what it could be?
Look below and you will see,
It is...

Answer: A monkey.

Ella Skidmore (5)
Westover Green Community School, Westover Green

Georgia's First Riddle

What could it be?
Follow the clues and see.

It looks **white and big**.
It sounds like *roar!*
It smells **fluffy**.
It feels **soft**.
It tastes **yuck**.

Have you guessed what it could be?
Look below and you will see,
It is...

Answer: A polar bear.

Georgia Gibbs (4)
Westover Green Community School, Westover Green

Carolina's First Riddle

What could it be?
Follow the clues and see.

It looks like **a sphere**.
It sounds like *crunch!*
It smells like **water**.
It feels **hard**.
It tastes **juicy**.

Have you guessed what it could be?
Look below and you will see,
It is...

Answer: An apple.

Carolina Nascimento-Carvalho (5)
Westover Green Community School, Westover
Green

Tayleanna's First Riddle

What could it be?
Follow the clues and see.

It looks **multicoloured**.
It sounds like **rain**.
It smells like **sweets**.
It feels **fluffy**.
It tastes like **lollipops**.

Have you guessed what it could be?
Look below and you will see,
It is...

Answer: A rainbow.

Tayleanna Imogene Mattock-Westlake (4)

Westover Green Community School, Westover Green

Ryvver's First Riddle

What could it be?
Follow the clues and see.

It looks **furry and brown**.
It sounds like **woof**!
It smells like **dirt**.
It feels **soft**.
It tastes like **meat**.

Have you guessed what it could be?
Look below and you will see,
It is...

Answer: A dog.

Ryvver Bastin (4)
Westover Green Community School, Westover Green

Bella's First Riddle

What could it be?
Follow the clues and see.

It looks like **a circle**.
It sounds like **a foam ball**.
It smells like **an apple**.
It feels **hard**.
It tastes **juicy**.

Have you guessed what it could be?
Look below and you will see,
It is...

Answer: An apple.

Bella Marie Gardner (4)
Westover Green Community School, Westover Green

Riley's First Riddle

What could it be?
Follow the clues and see.

It looks **brown**.
It sounds like *oooh!*
It smells **stinky**.
It feels **soft**.
It tastes like **bananas**.

Have you guessed what it could be?
Look below and you will see,
It is...

Answer: A monkey.

Riley Saunders (4)
Westover Green Community School, Westover Green

Ivy's First Riddle

What could it be?
Follow the clues and see.

It looks **black**.
It sounds like **a drum**.
It smells like **a bin**.
It feels **soft**.
It tastes like **blood**.

Have you guessed what it could be?
Look below and you will see,
It is...

Answer: A gorilla.

Ivy Rose Lewis (4)
Westover Green Community School, Westover Green

Lyle's First Riddle

What could it be?
Follow the clues and see.

It looks **yellow**.
It sounds like **yum, yum, yum**.
It smells **yummy**.
It feels **sticky**.
It tastes **yummy**.

Have you guessed what it could be?
Look below and you will see,
It is...

Answer: A banana.

Lyle Keats (5)
Westover Green Community School, Westover Green

Destiny's First Riddle

What could it be?
Follow the clues and see.

It looks **big**.
It sounds like **fireworks**.
It smells **dirty**.
It feels **soft**.
It tastes **not nice**.

Have you guessed what it could be?
Look below and you will see,
It is...

Answer: An elephant.

Destiny Demain (5)
Westover Green Community School, Westover Green

148

Kian's First Riddle

What could it be?
Follow the clues and see.

It looks **green**.
It sounds like *crunch!*
It smells **sweet**.
It feels **hard**.
It tastes **sweet**.

Have you guessed what it could be?
Look below and you will see,
It is...

Answer: A pear.

Kian Edward James Langdon (4)
Westover Green Community School, Westover Green

Isabela's First Riddle

What could it be?
Follow the clues and see.

It looks **yellow**.
It sounds **squishy**.
It smells **sweet**.
It feels **soft**.
It tastes **fruity**.

Have you guessed what it could be?
Look below and you will see,
It is...

Answer: A banana.

Isabela Lipinska (4)
Westover Green Community School, Westover Green

Ana's First Riddle

What could it be?
Follow the clues and see.

It looks **big and grey**.
It smells like **cake**.
It tastes like **a bush**.

Have you guessed what it could be?
Look below and you will see,
It is...

Answer: An elephant.

Ana Menyhart (5)
Westover Green Community School, Westover Green

YoungWriters®
Est. 1991

YOUNG WRITERS
INFORMATION

We hope you have enjoyed reading this book – and that you will continue to in the coming years.

If you're a young writer who enjoys reading and creative writing, or the parent of an enthusiastic poet or story writer, do visit our website **www.youngwriters.co.uk**. Here you will find free competitions, workshops and games, as well as recommended reads, a poetry glossary and our blog. There's lots to keep budding writers motivated to write!

If you would like to order further copies of this book, or any of our other titles, then please give us a call or order via your online account.

Young Writers
Remus House
Coltsfoot Drive
Peterborough
PE2 9BF
(01733) 890066
info@youngwriters.co.uk

Join in the conversation!
Tips, news, giveaways and much more!

f **YoungWritersUK**   🐦 **@YoungWritersCW**